Women
on

2. A lady driver and conductress in York, both smart and proud by their vehicle, prepare to take the Nessgate to Hull Road tram out, probably in 1916. Public transport very quickly became reliant on women staff and trams were no exception.

Introduction

The centenary of the outbreak of the First World War has focused many people's minds on the role their ancestors played in that conflict. This volume in the series attempts to cover the wide-ranging roles played by women from 1914-18 and highlight the bravery needed to carry out their duties, particularly at the front.

To cover the work of the many organisations created specifically for women volunteers would be impossible in this book; suffice it to say that most women who joined these organisations would have needed a relatively comfortable background as the cost of joining and their uniform would have been prohibitive to many. A number of the volunteers were allied to the Suffragette movement.

The role of postcards in illustrating the theatres of war and the lives of the people involved was immense. For many families it was the regular receipt of postcards that told them their loved ones were still alive. In these images we can see not only our ancestors in photo form but also the tasks that they undertook to support the war effort.

As well as showing the range of jobs that women undertook in the war, picture postcards focused on their role in helping recruitment. Patriotism demanded that everyone who could fight could be persuaded to enlist - until the adoption of conscription in 1916 made women's persuasive skills redundant.

It may be that the percentage of postcards depicting women war workers is very low compared to those of men, but postcard publishers never forgot the patriotism of re-inforcing the necessary work carried out by thousands of female volunteers. The postcards show that women were appreciated and that they could undertake many roles that had previously been deemed a male preserve. The way that women adapted to their new roles was to prove life-changing for them after the end of hostilities. Those roles in wartime can never be overstated, as postcards of the time so marvellously illustrated.

Michael Cox
Woodbridge, Suffolk
August 2014

Acknowledgments: I would like to thank my wife Jo, and Richard Hayes, for their help in the preparation of this book.

Front cover: The novelty of women working on public transport during the First World War inspired cartoonists to produce innumerable designs for postcards. Here Reg Maurice depicts a tram conductress dispensing tickets to passengers who include a small boy, a toff who'd deigned to enlist, and a soldier on leave. Card by the Regent Publishing Co. of London.

Back cover (top): Nursing on the move also involved ambulance trains, which were used to transport injured personnel from the front and at home. This card, published by Whorwell of Dover, shows the N5 ambulance train at Admiralty pier. The card was postally unused but has a description on the back of a nearby shelling. The two nurses are members of the Queen Alexandra Imperial Military Nursing Service (QAIMNS).

Back cover (bottom): Cartoonist Fred Spurgin shows Britannia as a siren inducing well-heeled men of various nationalities to flock to the flag to fight for Britain. This card, also published by Inter-Art (in their 'Beach' series), was posted at Malborough, Kingsbridge, in October 1915. Alice wrote on the reverse: " *Many thanks for card hope you will like this one isn't it nice...* " (then she mentions she's heard from various correspondents who've sent postcards)... " *Annie's card came in lovely for filling up my comic page & now I have started a patriotic page with a pretty girl that Winnie Boon sent me & an actress page in my album. We are both getting a nice lot now aren't we*". Postcards were the Twitter of the age, and the First World War stimulated tens of thousands of imaginative designs.

3. Many postcards were produced in art form, some by famous artists. Postcard illustrations showing work, professions or volunteer activities tend to fall into the following categories: uniformed and part of the military, uniformed and employed in essential services, the medical profession, factory workers and finally volunteers whose contributions were made with little or no sign of a uniform which makes it difficult to identify which service or organisation the women were employed in.

4. The postcard below shows Miss Sicele O'Brien, who originally came from Lohort Castle, Mallow, in Ireland. After the family came to England around 1912 Miss O'Brien became involved in voluntary work and shortly after the outbreak of war joined the First Aid Nursing Yeomanry (FANY) as an ambulance driver. FANY was set up in 1907 and in WW1 came under the control of the British Red Cross.

In 1916 Miss O'Brien was part of the St. Omer (Calais) Hospital Camp and around this time women were invited to help with ambulance driving to relieve fit and able men for other duties in the war effort. Miss O'Brien saw service all over the so-called Calais District and photos show her at Montauban, Albert and the famous area of battle at Vimy Ridge. After the war, Sicele became a celebrated aviator, winning air races at home and abroad. She crashed her plane at Mote Mount, Mill Hill, London in the 1930s and survived the impact.

5. The Women's Army Auxiliary Corps was formed in late 1916 and started active duty in 1917. Recruits were provided with their own uniform of a greatcoat, jacket, skirt and a badge with the initials WAAC. These women were employed both at the front and at home. The list of their duties was varied, but their main activity was to replace men as cooks, telegraphists, drivers, and mechanics. By 1919 nearly 60,000 women had become WAACs, with nearly 20% of them employed at the front. This portrait depicts Miss Edith Norden, and was taken in Rouen in December 1917.

6. In 1917 Queen Mary issued a statement relaying her appreciation of the wonderful work that the WAACs had carried out and she agreed to become Commandant in Chief. Subsequently, the WAAC was renamed Queen Mary's Army Auxiliary Corps and the uniform reflected this change until the Corps' disbandment in 1920-21.

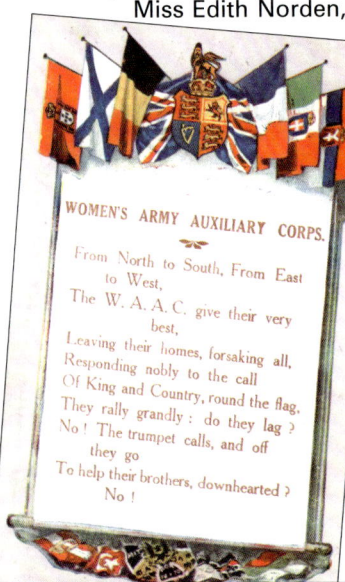

7. *(left)* Pretty girls, sometimes in uniform, were used on postcards to urge men to join the army, as on this postcard published by Silk & Terry of Birmingham. A note in the stamp box emphasises 'Entirely British production'. Most cards pre-war were printed in Germany.

8. Artist Arthur Butcher designed this encouragement to recruit postcard for the Inter-Art Publishing Co. It was posted to Blackpool from Weston, Derby, in July 1916.

Shooting Gallery, where Nurse Cavell was shot

9. Miss Norden served with the BEF, not only in Rouen - she appears to have moved around within the WAAC and subsequently the QMAAC. In her travels she went to the National Shooting Gallery in Brussels where Edith Cavell, one of the most famous nurses in WW1, was shot in 1915. This card is not dated but appears to be 1918.

10. When not at the Front, one of the favourite pastimes of soldiers was relaxing at an improvised music hall. Here Miss Norden is among a troupe, probably at Rouen, which entertained soldiers and those involved in the war effort.

11. A photo of members of the Women's Royal Naval Service (WRENS) by an unknown photographer. The WRENS were created in 1917 as a result of a shortage of manpower for active sea service, and disbanded in October 1919. Many jobs were shore-based and covered a variety of tasks including domestic duties. Over 6,000 women undertook these duties and were led by Dame Katherine Furse who led the first Voluntary Aid Detachment (VAD) to France in 1914. She was Commandant in Chief of the Joint Women's VAD in 1916. This card is unusual in that it illustrates two types of uniform, but just as important is the image of Dame Katherine, in the centre of the group at the back on the right.

12. Women's Volunteer Reserve (WVR) members outside the Drill Hall of the Queen's Westminster Volunteers, possibly in Fulham. As an organisation, the WVR had its roots in the Suffragette movement and emerged from the Women's Emergency Corps, which was set up in 1914. The founders were Decima Moore and Hon. Evelina Haversfield, who was a militant suffragette. It was expensive to join the WVR and probably only appealed to the upper classes. For example, a uniform jacket cost £2. Eveline Haversfield went on to be Chief of the Women's Reserve Ambulance Corps and became involved with The Scottish Women's Hospital Units set up by Dr Elsie Inglis.

13. This unused postcard is annotated on the reverse as being located at RAF Montrose and depicts the drivers who ran the motor transport. It probably dates around 1918-19. Montrose was the first operational military aerodrome in the UK. There is no indication as to which organisation these women belonged to as there were a number who provided drivers at home as well as at the front. The RAF was preceded by The Royal Flying Corps up to 1918.

14. In the uniform of the Royal Flying Corps, these two women are sitting on a Zenith motorbike which was manufactured in North London. The location is Upavon, Wiltshire, and the airfield there is sometimes regarded as the birthplace of the RAF. The card is not dated but this may be one of the earliest images of women employed in RFC duties. The two postcards on this page illustrate the role women played at airfields around the country in order to release men for operational duties.

15. This photo was taken in Lincolnshire and depicts women from the Forage Corps, two wearing the badge on their hats; the others, although wearing the same uniform, have different badges. One thing is clear - they are all wearing different hats!!

The Women's Forage Corps was set up in 1917 under the command of Superintendent Mrs Athole Stewart and enabled 6,500 soldiers to be released. The tasks the women undertook included hay-baling, sack-making, thatching, driving transport and clerical work.

16. (left) The need for large quantities of forage at the front necessitated additional labourers on the farms. In 1915, under the auspices of the Royal Army Service Corps, the War Office enrolled women to collect hay from farms and deliver to railway stations for onward movement to the front.

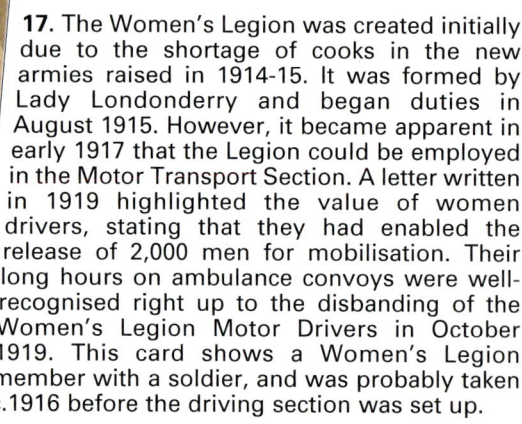

17. The Women's Legion was created initially due to the shortage of cooks in the new armies raised in 1914-15. It was formed by Lady Londonderry and began duties in August 1915. However, it became apparent in early 1917 that the Legion could be employed in the Motor Transport Section. A letter written in 1919 highlighted the value of women drivers, stating that they had enabled the release of 2,000 men for mobilisation. Their long hours on ambulance convoys were well-recognised right up to the disbanding of the Women's Legion Motor Drivers in October 1919. This card shows a Women's Legion member with a soldier, and was probably taken c.1916 before the driving section was set up.

18. An unused postcard annotated on the reverse as being Alice Meadows of the Women's Legion. She was Superintendent of 606 Company Motor Transport Army Service Corps.

19. A group of five women and a soldier are pictured on this card published by Fielder of Warminster. It is not possible to leave out canteen workers, even though it is difficult to identify the organisations they belonged to. There were so many different units, particularly from the upper social classes, that I can only guess that these women perhaps belonged to one of those. A Voluntary Aid Detachment nurse appears to be helping out.

20. This interesting image was taken at a prisoner-of-war camp in Groningen which housed the men from the 1st Naval Brigade who were taken prisoners. Its nickname was 'Engelse Kamp'. The ladies behind the counter are Miss Turner (on the left) and Mrs Coupland. The delights are priced in Dutch currency. The camp reputedly had a less strict regime than other POW camps, which resulted in British women being allowed to assist in the welfare of the internees.

21. A camp photo at Studland Bay, Dorset, probably c.1916. It depicts members of the Women's Sick and Wounded Convoy Corps. This organisation was raised by Mabel Annie Stobart and its aim was to serve near the field of battle as an emergency medical facility. Although seeing service in 1912, it was in 1914 that she set up a field hospital in Belgium. Mabel Stobart was not a suffragette, but she was a keen supporter of women's rights. The uniform has a distinct military look and this reflected how the organisation was run. Postcard images of members are somewhat scarce.

22. This unused postcard of women postal workers was probably taken early in WW1. The armband states 'Post Office Postman'. Later images show a more standard uniform for women, although the bags did not get any smaller!

23. The Fire Brigade demanded considerable support from women during WW1 as the men were required at the front. This card shows firewomen of the Preston, Lancashire, brigade. The women required a considerable amount of training before seeing active service.

24. The railways were an essential part of the war effort and required replacements for the men who were fighting at the front or driving the ambulance trains. These five women were employed as ticket collectors at Victoria Station. The card is dated 1915.

25. This series of postcards published by APS depicted various tasks and trades that were traditionally undertaken by men. These are two women railway carriage cleaners, an essential and labour-intensive task.

26. This postcard is one in a series of 'Life of Women in WW1'. The lady is pictured with her milk can and satchel for cash sales.

27. Well-represented on this postcard taken in 1918 are women employees of the bus and tram companies. Here are a group of 'clippies' with their inspector at an unknown location.

28. Flora White was a popular children's artist, and during the war turned her brush to patriotic designs, as did so many others. Here she uses a child to show the contribution women made to public transport. The card, published by The Photochrom Co. of London and Tunbridge Wells in their 'Celesque' series, was posted from Bettwys-y-Coed with the message "*How do you like this little girl - isn't she fat?*" [No - it's her uniform!].

29. An interesting card of men and women of Ipswich Corporation Transport. The men are motor men and the women are conductors. Most of the men appear to be quite older, which probably confirms the WW1 date of this unused card.

30. This very rare postcard was taken in the Holsminden prisoner of war camp. It shows five stewardesses of the Great Eastern Railways ship SS *Brussels* with two American nurses. Captain Fryatt, Master of the SS *Brussels,* was executed by the Germans in 1916.

31. Donald McGill's women were frequently portrayed as huge and overbearing. This one, on an Inter-Art 'Comique' series postcard, is determined to do her bit.

32. (top right) Published by Valentine of Dundee, Reg Carter's comic postcard creation shows a wartime madam in suitable attire - a shell and a sword for her hat, a patriotic all-enveloping dress, and a bulldog accesssory - the super-symbol of British wartime resistance. The caption also makes reference to the country's Dreadnought battleship.

33. Glamour artist William Barribal did his bit for the postcard war effort with this design published by the Inter-Art Co. The girl's egg basket is intended to emphasise home food production to combat the attacks on merchant shipping by German U-boats.

34. The Women's Police Service was originally set up by Margaret Damer Dawson and Mary Allen as the Women's Police Volunteers. They both had military leanings, but felt that women were much better equipped to deal with problems at home during WW1. This postcard shows F.W. Stolder, whose duties probably included screening women who were employed at the Gretna Munitions factory. This duty was carried out by many of the force of over a thousand women at the various munitions factories throughout the country.

35. An art card by Vivian Mansell of London depicts what many regard as an iconic image of a Land Girl. Many postcards were produced of women working on farms in the UK. However, a lack of annotation means that precise locations often cannot be identified.

36. An example of one of these uncaptioned images which still warrants inclusion shows different ages and dress of Land Army girls. This is probably East Anglia, and the women are working in a turnip field. The Land Army had its own magazine in WW1, '*The Landswomen*', which was continued in WW2 as '*The Land Girl*'.

37. A superb postcard published by Batchelder Bros. of Croydon which may have been a recruitment drive for women to join the Voluntary Aid Detachment (VAD), a joint nursing auxiliary service for those without formal qualifications. VAD was a joint organisation formed by the Red Cross and St John of Jerusalem.

38. Women were frequently shown on picture postcards persuading their husbands to volunteer for war service, though in reality the majority were distressed to see them leave. Many Donald McGill cartoons published by the Inter-Art Co. (this one is 'The Front' series no. 1225) had bi-lingual captions so they could also be sold in France, in this case a sub-title 'The Recruiting Sergeant'.

39. A fascinating 1916 image of the Fleet and District Ambulance (Hampshire) taken near Southampton Docks with Red Cross VAD men and women posing. Fifth from the left is Mrs Northcote, Commandant of the VAD Hants II Division. The card was sent by a VAD member, Thomas Quick.

40. This card is one of a series of WW1 images published by Bells of Westcliff, which were produced with a patriotic border. They had the advantage of being accurately captioned, identifying which of the hundreds of military hospitals in the UK was featured. This was one of the smaller ones, in Kelby, Lincolnshire.

41. Military hospitals at home often had entertainment and tea parties for the soldiers. This card shows one at Roslyn Lodge, Hampstead. The photo was taken in August 1916 and shows mainly Red Cross VAD nurses. The patients are wearing standard injured soldier's suits. Most are not wearing hats, somewhat unusual for outside images.

42. This scarce image shows women workers in the Belgravia Workrooms and War Hospital Supply Depot. They supplied hospitals around the UK and abroad. The uniform appears to be related to nursing but has no distinguishing marks.

43. This unused postcard depicts Sister Doughty of the Norfolk Tented Hospital. She is wearing the uniform of a QAIMN Reserve nursing sister and a Royal Red Cross medal, which could be a 1st or 2nd class, and also a silver service badge on her right lapel.

44. An art card by Wildt and Kray of the Royal Red Cross, described as a British Order of Distinction for Women and instituted in 1883. An associate would be awarded the 2nd Class version, mainly of frosted silver, whereas a member would have a 1st Class edged with gold. The 1st Class awards were made mainly at Buckingham Palace, a rewarding experience for women in the frontline of the medical service.

BRITISH ORDER OF DISTINCTION FOR WOMEN 1883

45. Another example of the Bells series of patriotic cards, this one of W. Horner, a Red Cross associated VAD nurse from one of the military hospitals in Burnley, Lancashire. Unlike the topographical cards by Bells, this series is not numbered, so it is difficult to assess the total number published.

46. A stunning image of the Great Eastern Hotel in Harwich, Essex, when it was occupied by injured soldiers and guarded by others. It is still a hotel and restaurant. The photo was taken by Steggles of Dovercourt.

47. An anonymously-produced postcard which shows an important part that women played in the life and history of Serbia in WW1. Dr Elsie Inglis, a Suffrage supporter in Edinburgh, was driven by the need for field hospitals in far-flung places which included Serbia. Eventually, over 1,000 women volunteered for service in around 14 fully-equipped hospitals. These women were in the 2nd Unit for Serbia and this image was taken prior to their departure from Cardiff.

48. A typical image from a UK military hospital, this one being Knighton VAD Hospital (Derbyshire). Soldiers often had their photos taken with the nurses caring for them. This is Nurse Tippetts with Thomson (at the back) who was a survivor of the *'Anglia'*, a hospital ship sunk by a mine when carrying over 400 injured soldiers from Calais to Dover on 17th November 1915. Many of the photos, when properly captioned, are important family history sources.

49. An important postcard taken in France of Sister (also Acting Matron) Ellen Baldry, who worked at some of the busiest military hospitals, including Rouen and Etretal. She is in the uniform of a Sister of Queen Alexandra Imperial Military Nursing Service. She received the Royal Red Cross 1st Class on 29th June 1918 from King George V at Buckingham Palace.

50. Another important postcard that shows the Stationary Hospital in Abbéville, France. This type of hospital, together with the general type, was known as a base hospital. They were located as near as possible to good transport links. Many of the nurses appear to be members of the QAIMNS and the officers could well be members of the Royal Army Medical Corps.

HE, SHE, AND IT.

51. There was a sustained campaign in British society during the war to vilify any able-bodied man who failed to enlist into the armed services, and picture postcards were at the forefront of it. Often, the 'shirker' was represented as a feckless toff, as on this postcard by Harold Earnshaw, published by Valentine of Dundee. The soldier's uniform has an irresistable appeal to the young lady. The role of women in these situations was hugely important in persuading men to 'do their duty', though in reality many women and girls actually tried to dissuade their sons, boyfriends and husbands from voluntarily enlisting.

STAFF-NURSE.
TERRITORIAL
FORCE
NURSING
SERVICE.

52. Although real photo cards are extremely important in illustrating the role of women in WW1, this art card shows a Staff Nurse in the Territorial Force Nursing Service, established in 1908 by R. Haldane. The uniform is not dissimilar to the QAIMNS but note the letter 'T' on the edge of the cape. The card is one of the 'National Series' of Patriotic Art Cards published by Millar & Lang of Glasgow.

53. Men in 'reserved occupations' doing important war work at home were issued with special armlets to show they weren't 'shirking'. This Bamforth postcard by their staff artist Douglas Tempest makes it plain, though, that any girl would prefer the 'real thing' in the person of an actual soldier rather than some stay-at-home pen-pusher. The use of children in adult situations was a common postcard ploy and enabled comic artists to say things they wouldn't have done with adult characters. This postcard was posted at Malmesbury in March 1916.

Women within the Suffrage movement and more widely were not pleased with the sentiments expressed on comic postcards during the war, regarding them as patronising.

54. This rather stern-looking lady is sub-Commander Mrs Kilroy Kenton of the Women's Reserve Ambulance Green Cross Society. They famously provided transport for the Red Cross during air raids, particularly in London. They were so accomplished they were attached to the Metropolitan Police for air raid defence.

55. This portrait is of Sister Charlotte Robinson, one of the most decorated women in WW1. Amongst the medals she was awarded was the Military Medal for courage and great personal risk when her stationary hospital in France was hit by four bombs. She rescued patients regardless of danger and showed magnificent coolness and resource. Charlotte was a career nurse and became Matron of Tidworth Military Hospital in 1937.

56. This postcard by Bromhead of Clifton depicts the Bandage Station where Red Cross workers rolled and packed dressings for use at home and abroad.

58. Another one of Bells' (Westcliff on Sea) patriotic cards, this one featuring A. Clark, a munitions worker at an unknown location.

57. Women munition workers were an essential part of the war effort. This 'Patriotic' postcard published by Birn Bros. of London was one of a series sold for 16 shillings a gross.

59. This group of munitions workers dated 1917 is unlocated, but the torpedo-like ammunition at the front makes it an interesting image for further research. The metal rings may provide the clue to the type of munitions they produced.

60. A scarce image of a woman welder munitions girl who worked at Parson's Motor Company in Southampton. The image was taken by Applins in the same town. The card is not dated but is probably 1917-18.

61. Voluntary aid worker on an artist-drawn postcard by Leonard Linsdell, published by Gale & Polden of Aldershot and posted in August 1917.

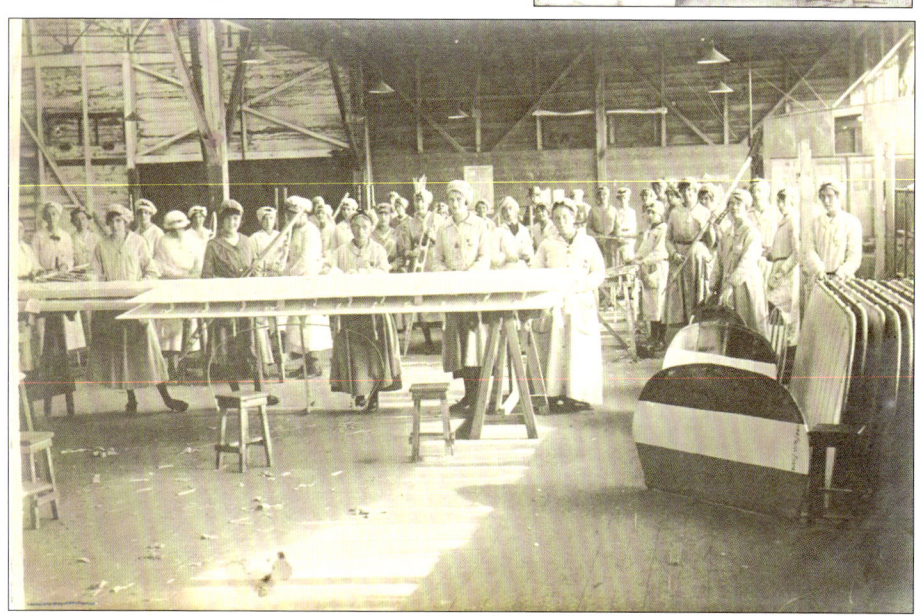

62. An aircraft factory in Poole, Dorset, appears to employ a considerable number of women. There is a large amount of plane wings on the right hand side. The photo dates from October 1918.

63. Hoffman Works in Chelmsford was famous in the area as a large employer for the manufacture of ball bearings, specialised work in which women played a major part. The postcard was published by Fred Spalding of Chelmsford.

64. Sphagnum moss is a spongy plant that absorbs moisture and has antiseptic qualities. It had been extensively used in Scotland for many years and this image shows a group of ladies making moss dressings at Kirkwall in 1917.

65. The Red Cross initiated many working groups and this one in Southwold, Suffolk, dated August 1914 is a good example. The ladies appear to be sewing garments apparently for volunteers who were supporting the war effort.

66. Flax has many uses for food, clothing or medicinal purposes. This long-stalked variety would probably be used for clothing. According to the message on the back of a photo of a Suffolk field, the flax the couple are picking 'For King and Country' was full of thistles. Painful work!

   Also important was the production and packing of turnips. The 'Turnip Winter' of 1916-17 saw the potato crop ravaged by bad weather, and food was supplemented by the increased crop of turnips. Extra volunteers were needed, forerunners of the Land Army formed in April 1917.

Pin-ups

67-71. The war also bred a new market for French artists such as Raphael Kirchner and Suzanne Meunier, who produced pin-up postcards, often with women in erotic poses, for the tommies in the trenches. They were intended to be kept, and few of these were ever posted. The male artists tended to use ladies close to their hearts as models for their artwork. In Britain, many artists leaned towards the patriotic theme by portraying glamorous ladies in relatively mundane tasks, maybe to appease the women's lobby, which wanted to see the work that women did recognised as equally important as that of the men fighting in the trenches. Illustrated here are postcards by artists Suzanne Meunier, 'Will', F. Fabiano and Maurice Pepin. All were published by Parisien firms.

72. A lot of baskets of different shapes and sizes with the caption 'Marylebone G.C. 25.6.17' indicates a railway connection, but there was a basket factory near the station in London. Images of the time show baskets being sent around the country via Marylebone station, which was owned by the Great Central Railway.

73. This rare photographic card is of Bentley's Brewery in Woodlesford, near Leeds in West Yorkshire. At the outbreak of war most of their male workers enlisted and left the production to women workers. The company's fortunes took a turn for the worse during the war due to a shortage of raw materials. The brewery was eventually bought out by Whitbreads, but was closed in 1984 and the buildings have since been demolished.

74. This image taken at an unknown location shows a group of women wearing a variety of uniforms. It was probably taken in a hospital laundry and the presence of only old men suggests it is WW1.

75. This photo was taken by the famous Fenland photographer Lilian Ream, whose career started at the age of 17, with her having her own studios in 1909. Inside this warehouse belonging to Smedleys in Wisbech, women workers are packing bottled foodstuffs.

76. There were so many charities raising funds in WW1 that they had to go further afield in their endeavours to collect money. This card was sent in 1915 to fundraisers in South Africa and shows the main shipping department of the Belgian Relief Fund, which was active in the UK. It was staffed by many women volunteers. Many of these charities were organised or founded by Suffragettes, or those with sympathetic leanings for women's rights.

77. This is another Belgian Relief Fund card, with a group of women collecting at Irthlingborough in Northamptonshire. You would probably have received a pin badge for any donation made, and each organisation/charity would have its own colours or emblems. This is a quality image by an unknown photographer.

78. This card was taken in London (Northern Millwall), the Limehouse entrance to Sufferance wharf. It shows women workers of C & E Morton Ltd., which produced mainly tinned foodstuffs. The company had other factories in the UK, including one at South Lowestoft close to the fishing industry. They provided and lost many men during the war, but all those lost were commemorated on the company's war memorials.

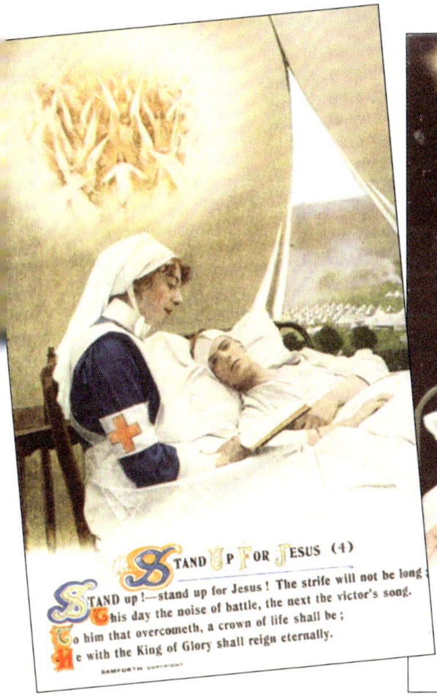

79-81. The postcard publishing firm Bamforth of Holmfirth in West Yorkshire produced huge numbers of song cards, many showing women as nurses.

82. Fund raising and charity flag days were an important part of life in WW1 and Queen Alexandra's involvement in hospitals featured all over the country. Her 'Rose Day', which was held in June, required distribution depots as illustrated here on this 1915 postcard. Street fund-raising was carried out mostly by woman, and heralded the introduction of charity flag events for every conceivable good cause.

83. This stall by the roadside features the sale of a wide range of goods including plumbing requisites. Captioned as 'Allies Day', the postcard, published by the Ipswich-based Earland, shows them raising money for charities such as the Belgian Relief Fund.

84. 'Remember our Wounded at the Front' is the theme of these fund-raisers on a day appropriately called 'Our Day'. On this occasion, the women are assisted by some elderly men at an un-named location on a Saturday in October (1915?) but they would probably have had more than one day for their worthwhile efforts.

85. The Kensington War Hospital supply depots distributed essential items hospitals required to treat soldiers, such as bandages, blankets and many other essentials. The operation began at 11 & 12 Kensington Square and rapidly overflowed to other houses. In 1915 there were over 1,000 volunteers a day, many working in a sterile environment.

86. As with any theatre of war, there were casualties, and numbers always included civilians and volunteers who were not part of the fighting front line, This fascinating headstone relates to Sister Violet Fraser, who was also remembered on the Dunbar War Memorial in Scotland. She may well have been a member of the Scottish Womens' Hospitals nurses who worked in Serbia. The grave and headstone were provided by the Serbian Relief Fund.